Th— All-Time Greatest
Film Songs

Published by
WISE PUBLICATIONS
8/9 Frith Street, London W1D 3JB, UK.

Exclusive Distributors:
MUSIC SALES LIMITED
Distribution Centre, Newmarket Road,
Bury St Edmunds, Suffolk IP33 3YB, UK.
MUSIC SALES PTY LIMITED
120 Rothschild Avenue,
Rosebery, NSW 2018,
Australia.

Order No. AM92045
ISBN 0-7119-4175-0
This book © Copyright 2005
Wise Publications,
a division of Music Sales Limited.

Cover photographs courtesy of Martin Philbey/Redferns and MPTV/LFI.

Printed in the EU.

YOUR GUARANTEE OF QUALITY
As publishers, we strive to produce every book to the highest commercial standards. The music has been freshly engraved and the book has been carefully designed to minimise awkward page turns and to make playing from it a real pleasure. Particular care has been given to specifying acid-free, neutral-sized paper made from pulps which have not been elemental chlorine bleached. This pulp is from farmed sustainable forests and was produced with special regard for the environment. Throughout, the printing and binding have been planned to ensure a sturdy, attractive publication which should give years of enjoyment.

If your copy fails to meet our high standards, please inform us and we will gladly replace it.

www.musicsales.com

WISE PUBLICATIONS
part of The Music Sales Group

London/New York/Paris/Sydney/Copenhagen/Berlin/Madrid/Tokyo

As Time Goes By

Words & Music by Herman Hupfeld

3

Bang Bang
(My Baby Shot Me Down)

Words & Music by Sonny Bono

bang, that aw-ful sound. Bang, bang, my ba-by shot me___ down.

Sea-sons came___ and changed the time,
Now he's gone, I don't know why. And

when I grew up I called him mine.
'til this day, some-times I cry.

He would al-ways laugh___ and say "Re-
He did-n't ev-en say good-bye. He

-mem-ber when we used to play?" Bang, bang, I shot you down. Bang,
did-n't take___ the time to lie. Bang, bang, he shot me down. Bang,

7

bang, you hit the ground. Bang, bang, that aw - ful sound.___ Bang bang, I used to shoot you
bang, I hit the ground. Bang, bang, that aw - ful sound.___ Bang bang, my ba - by shot me

down.

Mu - sic played and peo - ple sang,

just for me the church bells rang.

down.

Everybody's Gotta Learn Sometime

Words & Music by James Warren

Change your heart look a-round you._

Change your heart it will a-stound you._ And I

11

Ev-'ry-bo-dy's got-ta learn some-time, ev-'ry-bo-dy's got-ta learn some-time.

Ev-'ry-bo-dy's got-ta learn some-time. Mm, mm,

mm.

12

13

(Everything I Do) I Do It For You

Words by Bryan Adams & Robert John Lange
Music by Michael Kamen

1. Look in-to my eyes, _____ you will see, _____
2. Look in-to your heart, _____ you will find _____ there's

what you mean to _____ me. Search your heart, _____ search your
noth - ing there to _____ hide. Take me as I am, _____ take my

no love,___ like your love,___ and no___ oth - er, could give

more___ love. There's no - where___ un - less_ you're_ there, all the

time,_____ all the way,_ yeah._____

play 8 times, then fade

18

Goldfinger

Words by Leslie Bricusse & Anthony Newley
Music by John Barry

man with the Mi - das touch.___ A spi - ders touch.

Such a cold___ fing - er,___

beck - ons you_ to en - ter his web of sin. But don't go

in.

Gold - en words he will pour in your

20

cold. Gold - en words he will pour in your ear, but his lies_

___ can't dis -guise what you fear. For a gold -en girl_ knows when he's kissed her,

it's the kiss of death from Mis - ter Gold - fing - er.___

Pret - ty girl_ be -ware of this heart of gold.___ This heart is

22

Hopelessly Devoted To You

Words & Music by John Farrar

eyes are not the first to_____ cry._____ I'm

not the first to know there's just no get-ting ov — — er

you._____ 2. I

know I'm just a fool who's_____ will - ing_____ to
head is say-ing "Fool, for - get him."_____ My

no - where to hide   since you pushed   my love a - side._

_ I'm_____ out_____ of my head,

hope - less - ly de - vo - ted_____ to you._____

_ Hope - less - ly de - vo - ted_____ to

28

(I've Had) The Time Of My Life

Words & Music by Frankie Previte, John DeNicola & Donald Markowitz

30

sax. solo

(M) Now

I've   had   the time of my   life_____   no I nev - er   felt___ this way be-

34

35

I Will Always Love You

Words & Music by Dolly Parton

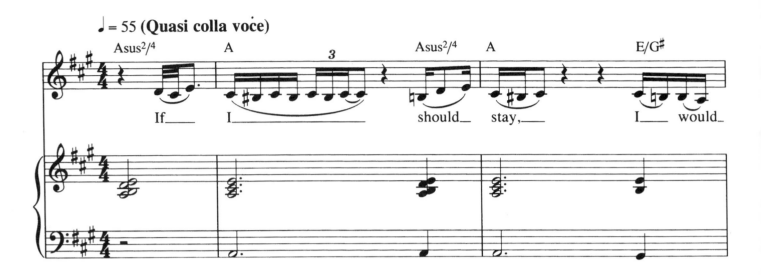

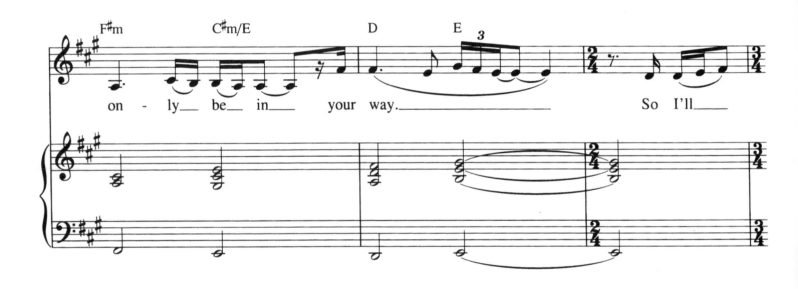

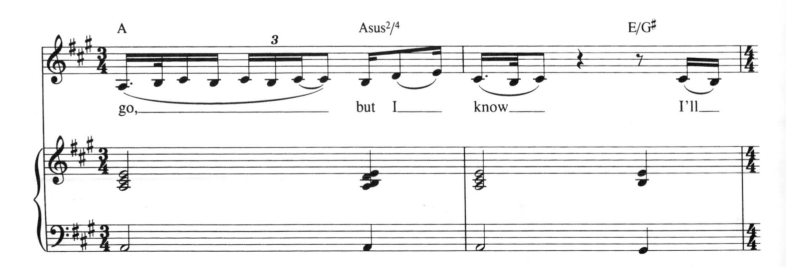

think of you__ ev - 'ry step__ of the way._____

a tempo (♩ = 60)

And I_____ will al - ways

love you,_____ I____ will__ al - ways

poco accel.

love you,_____ you,_____ my

37

40

41

Into The West
(from 'The Lord Of The Rings: The Return Of The King')

Words & Music by Annie Lennox, Howard Shore & Fran Walsh

43

And dawn will_____ turn_____ to sil - ver

glass.   A light on__ the wa - ter,

all   souls   pass.   pass   in - to__ the
2° grey   ships

West._____

Live And Let Die

Words & Music by Paul McCartney & Linda McCartney

say live and let die!_

Live and let die,_

live and let

die,_

live and let die._

To Coda ⊕

What does it mat - ter to ya,

when you got a job to do_ you got - ta

*8va lower ad lib till ***

do it well,_ you got-ta give the oth-er fel-low hell!_____

Love Is All Around

Words & Music by Reg Presley

1. I feel it in my fin-gers, I feel it in my toes.
(Verse 2 see block lyric)

The love that's all a-round me

and so the feel - ing grows.— It's

writ - ten on the wind, it's ev - 'ry - where I go,———

so if you real - ly love me, come on and let it show.—

51

You know I love you, I al - ways— will,— my mind's made up by the

way that I feel.— There's no be - gin - ning, there'll be no— end,— 'cause

on my— love— you can de - pend.

52

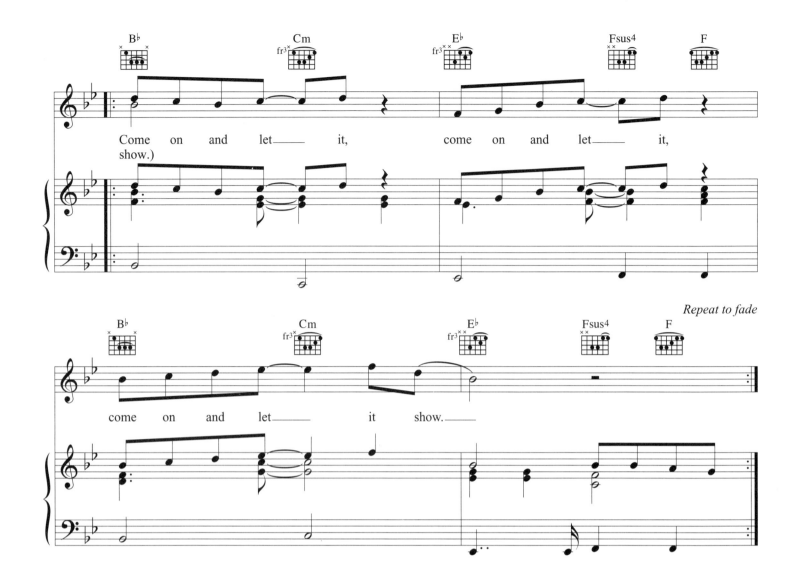

Repeat to fade

Come on and let____ it, come on and let____ it,
show.)

come on and let____ it show.____

Verse 2:
I see your face before me
As I lay on my bed;
I cannot get to thinking
Of all the things you said.
You gave your promise to me
And I gave mine to you;
I need someone beside me
In everything I do.

Mad World

Words & Music by Roland Orzabal

*Cello 2° only till ***

1. All a-round me are fa-mi-liar fa-ces, worn out pla-ces, worn out fa-ces. Bright and ear-ly for their dai-ly ra-ces,

2. Chil-dren wait-ing for the day they feel good, hap-py birth-day, hap-py birth-day. And I feel the way that ev-'ry child should

sad   that dreams in which I'm dy - ing are the best I've ev - er had.   I find it hard to

tell you,   I find it hard to take   when peo - ple run in cir - cles it's a ve - ry, ve - ry

mad   world.___   Mad   world.___

En - larg - en your___ world.   Mad   world.___

Mrs. Robinson

Words & Music by Paul Simon

60

We'd like to help__ you learn to help your -

- self.

Look a - round you, all__

__ you need__ are sym - pa - the - tic eyes.__

Stroll a - round__ the grounds__ un -

- til you feel at home.__ And here's to you__ Where have you gone_

Verse 2:
Hide it in a hiding place
Where no one ever goes
Put it in your pantry
With your cup cakes
It's a little secret
Just the Robinsons affair
Most of all you've got to hide it from the kids.

Koo koo kachoo Mrs. Robinson *etc*.

Verse 3:
Sitting on a sofa
On a Sunday afternoon
Going to the candidates debate
Laugh about it
Shout about it when you've got to choose
Every way you look at this you lose.

Where have you gone Joe Di Maggio
A nation turns it's lonely eyes to you
Ooh ooh ooh
What's that you say Mrs. Robinson
Jolting Joe has left and gone away
Hey hey hey
Hey hey hey.

My Heart Will Go On
(Love Theme From 'Titanic')

Words by Will Jennings
Music by James Horner

1. Ev - 'ry night in my dreams I see you, I
2. Love can touch us one time and last for a

Con pedale

Fm   E♭   D♭add9

You're   here,   there's   no - thing   I   fear___

E♭   Fm7   E♭

___ and   I   know___   that   my   heart___   will   go

D♭add9   E♭   Fm

on._____   We'll

E♭   D♭add9   E♭

stay   for - ev - er   this   way.___   You   are

68

Moon River

Words by Johnny Mercer
Music by Henry Mancini

Night Fever

Words & Music by Barry Gibb, Maurice Gibb & Robin Gibb

Moderate Disco beat

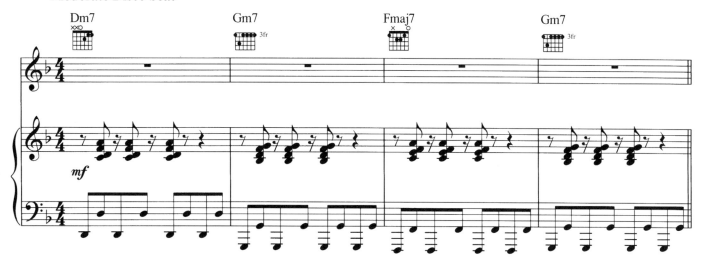

Lis - ten to the ground, there is move - ment all a - round. There is
heat of our love, don't need no help for us to make it. Gim - me

some - thing go - in' down, and I can feel it. On the
just e - nough to take us to the morn - in.' I got

waves of ___ the air, ___ there is danc - in' out ___ there. ___ If it's

fire in ___ my mind. ___ I got high - er in ___ my walk - in'. And I'm

some - thin' ___ we can share, we can steal it. And that

glow - in' in the dark; I give you warn - in.'

sweet cit - y wom - an, she moves through the light, _____ con -

trol - ling my mind ___ and my soul. _____ When you

Purple Rain

Words & Music by Prince

I nev-er meant 2 cause u — a-ny sor-row,

- er.

Pur - ple rain, pur - ple rain.

Pur - ple rain purple rain.

On - ly wan-na see u, on-ly wan-na see u in the pur - ple rain.

Raindrops Keep Falling On My Head

Words by Hal David
Music by Burt Bacharach

thing   I know___   the blues___ they send___ to meet

___ me   won't de - feat___ me.   It   won't be   long___   till

hap - pi - ness___ steps up___ to   greet   me.___

Rain - drops keep fall - in' on   my head,   but

Son Of A Preacher Man

Words & Music by John Hurley & Ronnie Wilkins

1. Bil - ly Ray was a preach - er's son_ and when his
(Verse 2 see block lyric)

dad - dy was preach - ing he'd come_ a - long; when they ga - thered round and start - ed talk - ing

cou - sin Bil - ly would take_ me walk - ing, through the back yard we'd go walk - ing,

then he'd look in - to__ my eyes,___ Lord knows to my_ sur - prise,_ the

on - ly one_ who could ev - er reach_ me was the son of a preach - er man._ The

on - ly boy_ who could ev - er teach_ me was the son of a preach - er man, yes he

was he was, mm, yes he was.

How well I re-mem-ber

the look that was in his eyes, steal-ing kiss-es from me on the sly.

Verse 2:
Being good isn't always easy
No matter how hard I try.
When he started sweet talking to me,
He'd come and tell me everything is all right,
He'd kiss and tell me everything is all right,
Can't get away again tonight.

Take My Breath Away

Words by Tom Whitlock
Music by Giorgio Moroder

Try A Little Tenderness

Words & Music by Harry Woods, Jimmy Campbell & Reg Connelly

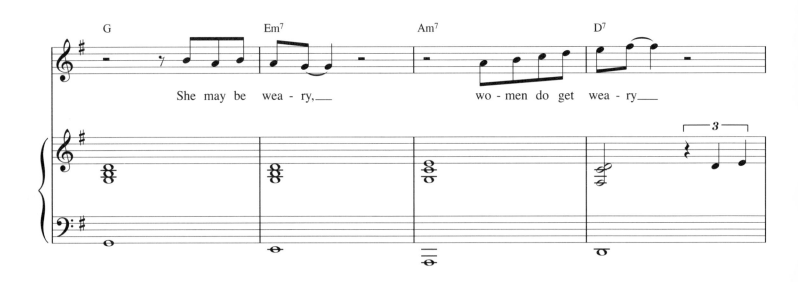

She may be wea - ry, wo - men do get wea - ry

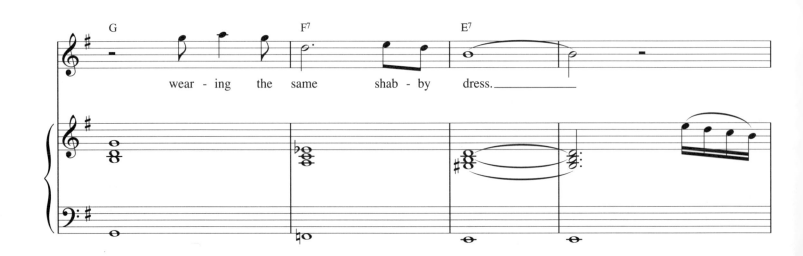

wear - ing the same shab - by dress.

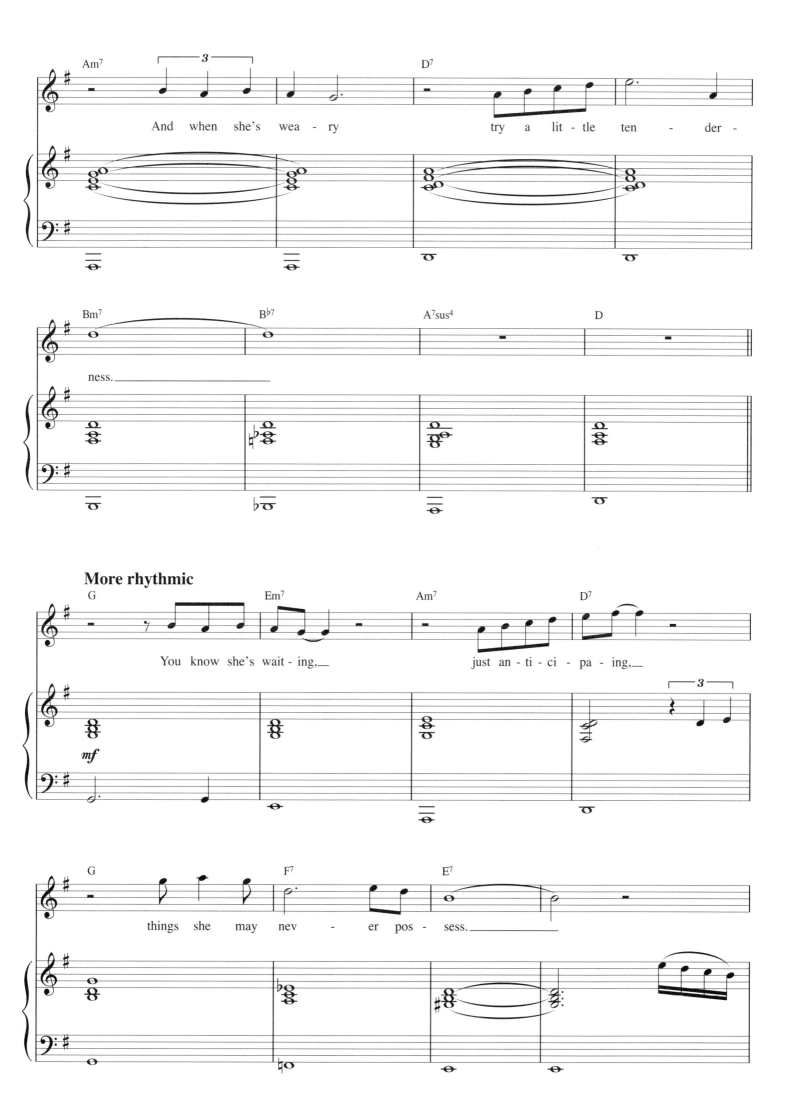

Unchain My Heart

Words & Music by Bobby Sharp & Teddy Powell

Original key A♭ minor

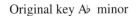

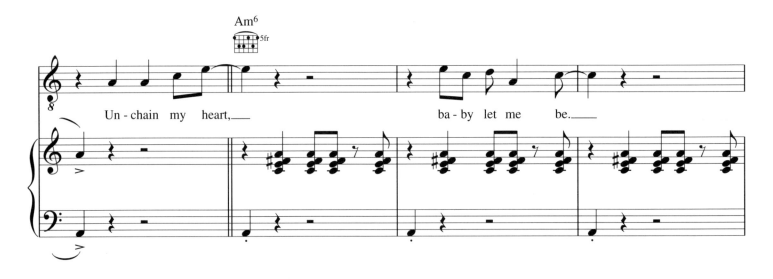

Un - chain my heart,____ ba - by let me be.____

Un - chain my heart,_____ 'cos you don't care a-bout me.

'cos you don't love me no more.

Ev - 'ry time I call you on the phone,

some fel - la tells me that you're not at home,_ so un - chain_ my heart, oh

please, please set me free._____ I'm un - der your spell

Unchained Melody

Words by Hy Zaret
Music by Alex North

Up Where We Belong

Words & Music by Jack Nitzsche, Will Jennings & Buffy Sainte-Marie

road   is ___ long.   There are moun-tains ___ in our ___ way, ___

but we {climb   a} step   ev-'ry day.
        {climb them a}

Love lift   us   up where we   be- long, ___   where the

ea- gles   cry _____   on a   moun - tain high.

115

When You Say Nothing At All

Words & Music by Don Schlitz & Paul Overstreet

1. It's a - maz - ing how you can speak right to my heart,
(Verse 2 see block lyric)

with - out say - ing a word

truth in your eyes say-ing you'll— nev-er leave— me. The touch of your hand says you'll catch

____ me when-ev-er I fall.____

You— say it best when you say no-thing at all.____

when you say no-thing at all.—

120

me when - ev - er I fall.

You say it best when you say no - thing at all.

(You say it best when you say no-thing at all.)
(female vocals)

(You say it best when you say

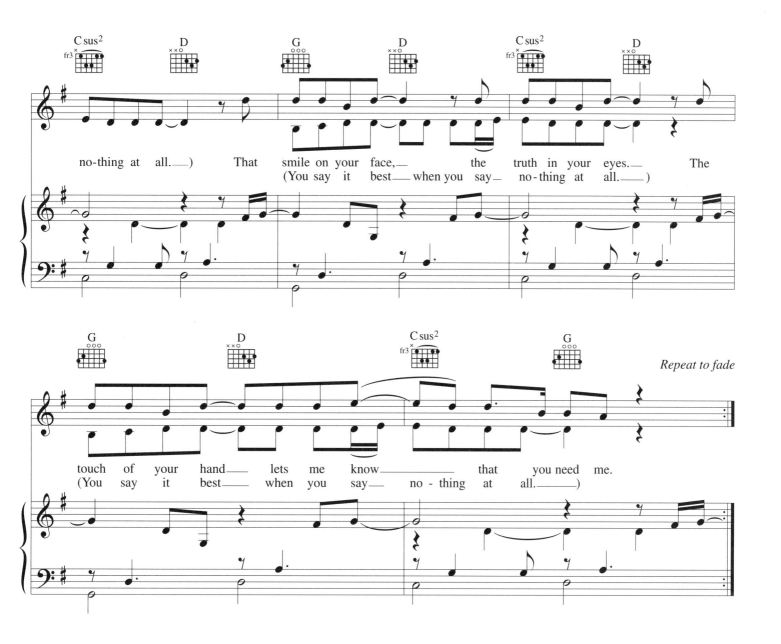

Verse 2:

All day long I can hear people talking out loud
But when you hold me you drown out the crowd
Try as they may they can never defy ~~define?~~
What's been said between your heart and mine.

The smile on your face *etc.*

Your Song

Words & Music by Elton John & Bernie Taupin

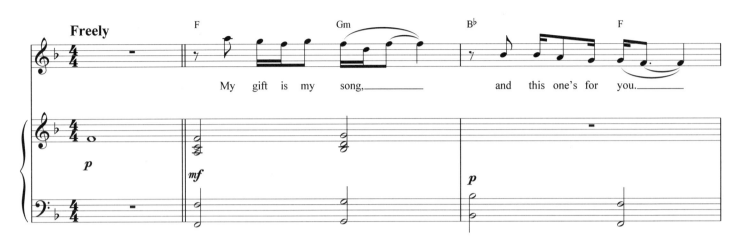

My gift is my song,_____ and this one's for you._____

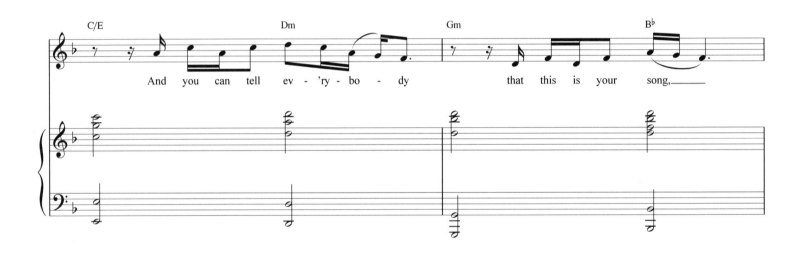

And you can tell ev - 'ry - bo - dy that this is your song,_____

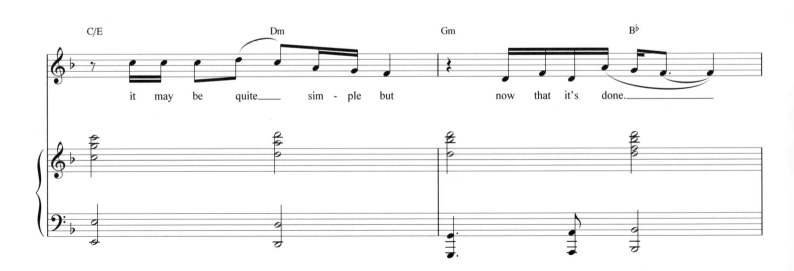

it may be quite____ sim - ple but now that it's done._____

It's for peo - ple like you that____ keep it turned on.

So ex - cuse me for - get - ting,____ but these things I do,_____ you see I've for - got - ten if_ they're green

_ or_ if they're blue. But well the thing is, what I real - ly mean,

yours are the sweet - est eyes_ I've_ ev - er seen.____

cresc.